LAVA LAMP DREAMS

BY
BLAKE STERLING

Please visit the author's Instagram
@ Sterling_Poetry
to find out more information

DEDICATION

First off, I would like to thank everybody who is taking time out of their lives to get a little taste of my crazy. I wrote these poems while going through some of, if not the, hardest times in my life. There is love, sadness, depression, deep thoughts and crazy artistic views from my mind.

This is my life and it feels like the opposite of how most people view theirs.
I hope you feel.
Enjoy.

This book is broken into sections.
I wrote certain poems in certain places and I wanted to make sure that you, the reader, knew that. I felt like if you knew where I was when I wrote, that it would give you a little more insight into my state of my mind.

Plus, it didn't feel right to throw all the poems one after the other with no sort of rhyme or reason. I hope you enjoy them.

HEARTBROKEN iN BED
5:OO 4M

Everybody has gone through some sort of heartbreak in their life.

This is my chapter of that.
Heart break, sadness, and wanting to learn to love again.

HEART BREAK

Two people
Two hearts
Three pieces
One loved
One lied
One cheated…

YOU'RE SUCH AN EASY TARGET

Looking from the outside in, You're falling apart
Slowly separating from reality
Quickly approaching guilt
I consume you

Thinking of me and only me
You try to get your mind off of me
But I'm everything you see
I run your life, your mind

You are mine
Sleep, You can't
You are in my possession
I am depression

SOLAR ECLIPSE

I want a certain kind of love
A love that only comes so often
A love as a rare as a solar eclipse

GALAXY

I would go to the farthest galaxy
Just to find the smallest missing piece
Of your healing heart

SCREAMING!

I like to scream underwater
Where no one can hear me
But the seaweed
Tickling my feet

YOUR EYES

I stare into your eyes and see so much more than you
think
I see more than just the bluish green tint
I see the yellow glow from the very back,
Trying to fight its way to the front

I see the black outlines that get overlooked because
they aren't bright
I see more than color, more than detail
I see your life story
I see the hurt you've felt in your past, the joy you feel
in the present

When I look into your eyes
I see so much more than color
I see...
Life

<u>BREAK</u>

I'm internally soaked from my mental tears
I've been holding them in for so many years
I'm going to…
Break soon.

SiTTiNG iN MY CAR
3:13 AM

I wrote this during such a quiet night.
It was pitch black outside with a deep red tint coming from under the seat of my car.
This was a sad night with a little hint of beauty mixed in.

REALIZATION

I'm not okay
And that's okay

IMPERFECTION

You weren't meant to be perfect
So stop trying to be

SCARED OF EVERYTHING

I'm scared of life
I'm scared of death
I'm scared of sitting here taking this deep breath

I'm scared that I'll lose
I'm scared of what to choose
I'm scared of everything

I'm scared of you

THE FLOWER

The flower is like us
Personalized in
Color
Size
And type

Just like humans, every flower must die
Out of air to breath
Out of water to drink
The flower lays to rest

Every petal has fallen
Like every person who has ever stood
The flower is beautiful
But the flower is no more.

<u>SILENCE</u>

Silence is beautiful
Like the curves on a woman
Or the reflection of the sun hitting a wave

CRAVE

You are everything I crave
You're a perfect mixture of my happiest thoughts
And deepest demons

THOUGHTS AT THE OCEAN
12:17 AM

Still trying to move on and drunk.
I think that makes it at least five times worse.
I can't deny it though, I was getting better.

LOVE AT THE OCEAN

As the waves and wind naturally occur
I can't help but feel healed
I close my eyes and listen to the water
And let go
I can't see anything
But you don't need your eyes
when you're looking with your heart

LETTING GO

The ocean is the best listener you can find
As the wind feels like bullets blowing through my hair
I kamakaze my feelings into thin cold air
The ocean is the best listener you can find

LIGHTS AT THE END

There is no light at the end of the tunnel
But there is light surrounding the darkness the tunnel
makes for you

The ocean will forever have light
The sun, moon, and city lights make it possible

Tunnels don't reflect the positive light trying to fight
into your life
But the ocean constantly makes it for you

SOMETIMES I CRY

Sometimes I cry just to feel my tears
Not because I'm sad…
But because I want to remember

DROWNING

I drown in my emotions and not in my sorrows

HIDE AND SEEK

Sometimes I like to play hide and seek with my feel-
ings
Not because I don't like being found
But because I don't want to seek

CRACKLE

The core of a fire dying on coal
The coal keeping the fire alive
Like a man to a woman
And a woman to a man
Two souls you can not divide

SUMMER NIGHT

Starry nights on a summer trip
A big lake and a naked dip
Alcohol pressing the bottom of your lip
A night you won't remember but will never forget

SENSITIVE

Men are sensitive
We have a rocky covering with a lava core

MARIN HEADLANDS
8:14 PM

Let me tell you that it was FREEZING when I came
here tonight.
It was also almost 8 months since the beach.
I had gone a while without writing cause I had lost
feeling.
Then she gave it back.

LOST AND FOUND

Lost in your words
Found in your eyes
Lost in your voice
Found in your mind

Lost in the way your body moves
Like a blade of grass blowing in the wind
Found in the way your heart beats
Like drums echoing through the streets

FOG

The fog rolls in like a bowling ball striking pins
Quick, powerful, and precise
As it covers the hills in its grey blanket
You can't help but notice the beauty in something so
simple

Water vapor getting pushed by wind
Covering every single object in its path
Not destroying or staying on
Gently gliding over
Simply saying hi, then bye

CHANGE

I'll be the wind for your sail
I can be a bed for your rest
I'll be anything you need
If you're a bird, I'm a bird
If you're a tree, I'm a tree
I'll change for your every need

I'VE NEVER LIVED

I've never lived
Only existed
Then I met you
And you changed everything

<u>SMILE</u>

Her smile makes my heart smile
And it's as simple
And as complicated as that

LOVING YOU

My favorite hobby is loving you,
My Queen

<u>WILD SIDE</u>

She's a beautiful old soul
But she's got that wild side too
And it's fucking crazy

<u>PAINTED ON A CANVAS</u>

Painted on a canvas
The red of the Golden Gate
The stars in the back looking more and more fake

The Complexity of a Simple Mind

This is me.
This is my mind.

PASSION IS DEEPER

Passion is deeper than just wanting to be with her
It's deeper than saying you love her
Passion is feeling your souls and bodies connect

It's feeling her when she's miles away
Listening to her when she's not talking
Seeing her when she isn't there

You say you're passionate
But ask yourself
Can you see her right now?

ANTS AND HUMANS

Ants work for their queen
Humans work for their president
Ants will rebuild when their hill gets tampered with
Humans rebuild when we get cracked surfaces

Ants will fight together to keep themselves safe
Humans will do the same
There aren't many differences between ants and humans...
But there is one that truly sticks out to me

Ants will live, love, and die together
It really doesn't matter how different any ant is
The ant could have two less legs and one less antenna...
The ant would still be considered as an equal in their tribe

Can we say the same?

LOVE LETTER TO YOU

You drive me wild in the best ways
Sometimes we may not ride the same waves
And we could have different on and off days
Your eyes glisten like the waves of the ocean, while
the sun is setting
in the back
Your smile is picture perfect
That's why every picture you're in is perfect
Your lips are addicting, almost a necessity
Your skin is softer than freshly dropped snow in the
winter
Your imperfections make you perfect
When you are you
I feel our love is true

LOVE

Love is stronger than anything in this world
It could tear you down in a matter of seconds
And build you up in the same time
Love is a lot more than just a word
It's an action
Something you have to prove
Love is an imperfect groove
Love is the way 2 dancers move
Love is how I feel about you
And I'll prove it everyday if I have too

ROBOTS

I have a number
I have a class
I have a birth year
And I'm never last
I do what they tell me
Cause that's what we do
We're robots in society
Oh, whoopty do
I clean and I cook
I can write and read a book
I go to school for years upon years
To realize I should have picked different careers
When you realize you're a robot just following the path
It's always a little late To stop the crash
You crash into another robot
One you used to be like
You try to tell it to stop and listen
Maybe take a look around
But it doesn't- it just keeps its head down
We're robots in society
We don't have any say
We sit back and watch
And just say OK
We're robots in society
They give us our parts
They make us more smart
But never do we see
That we are all in one dream
It may not be ours
But if you look so very far
You can see your dream
And if you try your hardest you just might make it
Be one of the few who doesn't have to take it
A robot in society no more
Living your life to the fullest
That's not a chore

FLOATING

I'm floating in space
But I'm not a comet
And no, no, I'm not an asteroid
I'm not a star of a planet
But something else
That's everywhere
i'm a color that's hated
A color that will never be faded
I make everything possible
I'm the reason you're alive
I am black matter
I am dark and I am cruel
According to everyone, my color defines me
So what did I do wrong
You hate me for nothing
But you should love me for everything
Because it's not white matter that keeps the world
running
It's black

WINE GLASS

A party
8 people, a perfect ratio
4 girls, 4 guys, one night
Drinking games and loud music
A lot of laughs and so much tension
Sexual tension between couples
Singles, everyone
A wine glass hits the floor
It shatters into a million pieces, never being found again
Everyone keeps dancing, not even knowing that the glass
has broken
I'm broken, but nobody notices
They are always dancing
Too busy to notice that I'm not here right now
That I'm shattered and can't feel my own heart
I want them to look, to care, to find me
But they never do
A party
Going on all night
A wine glass broken like the back porch light
Shards of me slipped into the grass
Forgetting about me as they pass
I'm like a ghost, but everyone can see me
But really no one can see me
They don't understand my mind
My thoughts
They look at me and see a perfect human
Standing tall, confident, no problems
But here I am
Broken
At a party
Going on all night
A wine glass broken like the back porch light
I
Am
The
Wine
Glass.

A GUN

A gun rests in the hands of a dead man
A suicidal man who really had no plans
He would wake up every morning
Brush his teeth, put on his clothes

He would drive until it got dark
And sit in his car with the gear in park
Looking at the sunset slowly but surely setting in the
distance
He thinks

He thinks all the wrong things
About how he's one in a billion people
And if he even matters or if he's even going to make a
difference in the world
He contemplates this every night

Driving home from his repeated day
He listened to a song that made him feel gray
He got home and thought, why does it make me feel
that way
The man tried to think about the positives in life

He found nothing
So he went to his bed, felt under the pillow
He grabbed the gun that would take his life
The gun whispered
Hello

SIMPLE BEAUTY

Beauty does not sit or rest
It simply follows you until you undress
Because beauty isn't defined by the naked breast
It's the heart underneath that makes you look the best

GLOW

Out of the deepest darkest forests in your mind
The cells falling like heavy drops of rain in the ama-
zon
To loud, can't think
To quiet, can't talk

The sun splits the leaves
The water drips down the trees
Light and liquid combine on the backs of the bees
wings
GLOW

DO YOU WANT TO KNOW

My darkest secret is hidden deep beneath the surface of my steady beating heart… When it stops you can have it
Sincerely, me

BED

In bed with you next to me is all I want
I'm content
I'm at peace
I feel…
I feel loved
I forgot how that felt till I met you

ASSISITED SUICIDE

She broke his heart
Slowly took him apart
And then left

He can't live without her
He has his hand on the trigger...
He pulls

The phone rings for what seems like an eternity

THE BRIDGE

The bridge standing tall and muscular
The metal and nails getting worked everyday
Cars running over the heart
Makeshift tattoos on his body

The simple bridge growing older everyday
His legs shaking from standing in the water for so
many years
The top slowly rolling away from so many of gods
tears

It's the bridges time
As he collapses he knows it's not because he was
weak or fatigued
It was because of the power and damage The other has
created to tear him down

The bridge is more than just a huge hunk of metal
The bridge is a gateway to a better place
Find yours…
And build it

Thank You

Thank you to everybody who read this! I feel like I'm taking a huge risk by putting my feelings out there, but no risk no reward, right?

To everybody who is supporting me, I am so grateful for you.

I want to thank my family for always supporting me, no matter what I do.

My Dad, my brother Ach, and my Mamma, I owe you everything.

About the Author

Blake Sterling is the son of New York Times Best - Selling author, J. Sterling. He currently lives in California. This is his first collection of poems, but won't be his last. For more information on Blake, please follow him on Instagram at @sterling_poetry